Encounter Christianity

In Journeys about Jesus

Alan Brown and Alison Seaman

**The National Society (Church of England)
for Promoting Religious Education**

❖
Support for all involved in Christian and Religious Education
❖
RE resource centre in London
❖
Training courses and conferences
❖
Training and support for Section 23 Inspectors
❖
A wide range of publications for all involved in Christian education
❖
An extensive archive on the history of the Church in education
❖
Websites on Collective Worship, www.natsoc.org.uk, and
RE and Management of Church schools, www.churchschools.co.uk

For further information please contact:
The National Society, Church House, Great Smith Street, London SW1P 3NZ.
Tel: 020 7898 1518   Email: info@natsoc.org.uk

How does she feel?

How do **you** feel
when you are
on your own?

Rejection

The travellers, weary now in every pore
with eyes downcast beneath the darkening sky
still wait in silent hope outside the door.

The inn is full; they've seen it all before.
We've no room here! and then a brusque *Goodbye!*
to travellers weary now in every pore.

In disbelief, too tired to implore,
they try to turn away but wonder why
they wait in silent hope outside the door.

Rejection is not easy to endure;
where *can* you go when there's no place to lie
for travellers weary now in every pore?

The landlord hesitates, becomes unsure,
now sensing a despair he can't pass by;
they wait in silent hope outside the door.

The *stable*? Could he offer only straw
with lowing cattle for a lullaby?
The travellers, weary now in every pore,
wait still in silent hope beside the door.

Poem by Judith Nicholls

Are there times
when you want to be
on your own?

Sometimes we choose
to be on our own.

Jesus chose to
spend time alone.

When we make a journey ...

who protects us
from danger?

8

The Bible tells how the
Israelites escaped from Egypt.

They believed God was
their guide and protector.

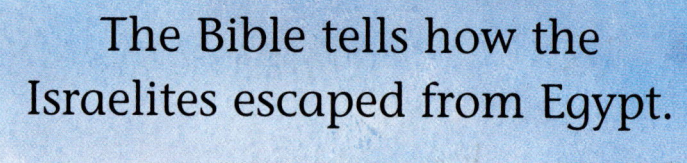

Who guides and protects **you**?

Messages

Angels trod through Jacob's dreams,
stole behind his sleeping eyes;
with soundless steps they rose, descended,
rose, descended, still ascended,
never pausing on the ladder
stretching to the watching skies.

Angels trod through Jacob's dreams,
messengers in dream-disguise.
When they try to warn or guide
inside *our* dreams, shall we just hide
or welcome them with seeing eyes?

Poem by Judith Nicholls

Welcome back!

How does it feel
to come home?

What do you do when you are thrilled about something?

King David danced for joy when he brought the Ark home to Jerusalem.

Jesus also came home to Jerusalem.

He was welcomed like a king.

How do **you** welcome a special visitor?

Where are they going?

Who has been this way?

Christians believe that Jesus shows the way and they try to follow in his footsteps.

Who do you go
to when you
are afraid?

Christians believe
that Jesus is
like an anchor
in a storm.

What gives you
confidence to do things
on your own?

The Bible tells that
Jesus went to heaven.

He promised his disciples
the gift of the Holy Spirit
to help them follow
in his footsteps.

About each picture

Pages 2–3 When a child feels lonely

Background

If life is a journey, then loneliness is the slow boat on that journey. Virtually all pupils will have experienced loneliness and one is often even more lonely in the presence of others. What emotions about loneliness lie in the hearts and minds of pupils? Loneliness is not about being on one's own, it is a feeling of being unwanted and isolated in the context of other people's friendship and sociability.

Ways of using the picture

✤ Discuss loneliness with the pupils. How do they feel? How do they cope with it?

✤ Do they see another person's loneliness and how do they try to help?

✤ How can pupils (and adults) break into another's loneliness sympathetically? How can we try to break the cycle of loneliness?

Bible references: *Luke 15.11-32, 1 Kings 19.11-13*

Pages 4–5 Joseph and Mary find a place to stay

Background

You have to make a long journey, a long and uncomfortable trek; you look forward to arriving but a door slams in your face. You have to 'make do'. This story, from Luke's Gospel, is re-lived today in the refugees and the homeless, but most of us have 'travelled' in body or mind to be turned aside to 'make do with the stable'. This well-known, romanticized story is a powerful example of rejection at the end of a journey, as reflected in Judith Nicholls' poem.

Ways of using the picture

✤ Have the pupils ever been in a similar situation – nowhere to stay or at the end of a tiring day? Do they look forward to their bed in their home?

✤ Look up Nazareth and Bethlehem on a map. Estimate the distance and how long the journey would take at walking pace. How might Joseph and Mary have felt?

✤ Discuss how refugees must feel as they flee from their countries, seeking safety and security.

Bible reference: *Luke 2.1-7*

Pages 6–7 Jesus in the desert

Background

Jesus went off into the wilderness for forty days, so the Bible says, to reflect on his future life. What would be the best way to teach, so that people would understand and accept his message? He chose to be alone, giving himself time to think what his life might hold. What would he teach? How would he and others react? Would there be pain or even death? He was tempted by the devil to take the easy way, to become a miracle worker to ensure that people would believe he was the Son of God. Jesus rejected the temptations. He wanted people to arrive at their own conclusions about him, not accept him unthinkingly.

Ways of using the picture

✦ How often do the pupils want to be on their own? Where do they go if they want to be alone? What do they think about?

✦ Use Stanley Spencer's painting to discuss with the pupils what they think would be in Jesus' mind during forty days in the desert.

✦ What tempts pupils? How easy is if for them to resist temptation? How easy is it to fail?

Bible references: *Matthew 4.1-11, Mark 1.12-13, Luke 4.1-13*

Pages 8–9 Crossing the road

Background

The journey is one of the great themes in literature. In epic stories, there is always excitement, adventure and, most of all, danger. In the journeys children and adults make, there is danger too; it could be danger from traffic, losing one's way, even missing the last train or bus. Today, dragons and evil whirlpools are not common dangers as they are in stories. Society builds in ways of protecting us from the dangers of our journeys. We all look for guidance and protection on our journeys.

The pupils will make lone journeys – to school, to the shops, to friends and relations. All of us can feel insecure about our journeyings.

Ways of using the picture

✦ Discuss with the pupils who protects them on a journey. Why do they need someone to help them cross the road?

✦ Who or what do they need to be protected from on a journey?

✦ How do pupils and their parents strike a balance between allowing freedom and providing enough protection?

Bible reference: *Psalm 23*

Pages 10–11 The Israelites in the desert

Background

The Israelites fled from Egypt, after centuries of slavery, under the leadership of Moses. The Egyptians had finally let them go after suffering ten dreadful plagues, but where were they to go, who would protect them? The Bible story says God provided a 'pillar of cloud by day' and a 'pillar of fire by night' for the Israelites to follow. For forty years, they needed protection from starvation, thirst and assault. None who started out reached the Promised Land, so when they reached Canaan, it was a new start, a new beginning.

Ways of using the picture

✤ What great journeys do people undertake – to the South or North Pole, sailing around the world? What protection do they need and how do they find the way?

✤ Forty years is a long journey for these refugees. What problems would they have? How would families cope?

✤ Imagine living life as a nomad, constantly on the move. Would life change?

Bible reference: *Exodus 13.21-22*

Pages 12–13 Jacob's dream

Background

Dreams can be pleasant events or nightmares. Biblical characters often received messages from God in dreams, messages that they accepted as true. Examples in the Bible include the dreams of Joseph, Samuel, Joseph (Jesus' father) and the Magi. Could Jacob's ladder be the stairway to heaven? Jacob thought the place was sacred and so he renamed it 'Bethel' – 'House of God'. Look at how John Reilley captures this in his painting. How can dreams allow us to explore some of our deepest feelings?

Ways of using the picture

✤ Discuss pupils' dreams. Do they know they dream? Are they vivid, recurring dreams? Would a dream change their lives?

✤ Some people today are 'warned' in dreams. Do the pupils accept this? Does it mean that events are fixed and cannot be changed?

✤ Read Judith Nicholls' poem and look carefully at the picture. What do the pupils think the last three lines might mean?

Bible reference: *Genesis 28.10-22*

Pages 14–15 Welcome home!

Background

The Israelites made a number of promises to God, promises that they failed to keep. Each time, God welcomed them back with open arms. Some of the themes of the Bible are transgression, apology, reconciliation, discipline and self-discipline. One of the best-known stories in the New Testament is the Parable of the Lost Son. His father welcomed him back with open arms – but did his older brother? God, in Christian belief, always has open arms, welcoming home the traveller.

Ways of using the picture

✢ Coming home – who or what do the pupils look forward to seeing?

✢ We come home to: a house, grandparents, parents, people who care, a place, a town – the familiar. What are the pupils' experiences of coming home?

✢ Read the Parable of the Lost (or Prodigal) Son. What do the pupils think would be the feeling of the son, the father and the elder son? What do they think would happen next?

Bible reference: *Luke: 15.11-32*

Pages 16–17 David dances into Jerusalem bringing the Ark home

Background

The Israelites had been in the wilderness for forty years, and centuries in the Promised Land before King David brought the Ark to its home, Jerusalem. The Ark of the Covenant represented the presence of God amongst the Israelites. It was holy and treated with great veneration and deep respect and had been carried with the Israelites on their travels. David was fulfilling God's command. He believed Jerusalem would be the resting place for God; Israel would have a place to worship God as they should. God would be home in Jerusalem after years of travelling. David danced with joy when he brought the Ark to Jerusalem where it would later rest in the Temple that his son, Solomon, would build.

Ways of using the picture

✢ What makes the pupils want to 'dance with joy'?

✢ What does it feel like to come home, at the end of school or at the end of the holidays?

✢ Why do the pupils think David was so happy to be bringing the Ark into the capital city? What did it represent to him and to the Israelites?

Bible reference: *2 Samuel 6.12-19*

Pages 18–19 Jesus enters Jerusalem

Background

The Gospels vary on whether Jesus went to Jerusalem once or three times during his ministry. When Jesus entered the city, in the week of his death, he did so on a donkey. He was a king, for those who believed, yet he entered the city as a humble traveller, arriving home in peace and humility. The day is called 'Palm Sunday' because crowds welcomed him, throwing palms in his path. Jesus was teaching his followers the importance of humility and trying to demonstrate what type of 'king' he was.

Ways of using the picture

✤ How do pupils expect that a king should enter a city? What did entering on a donkey symbolize?

✤ Could Jesus' entry into Jerusalem be paralleled with a football team coming home with a trophy? Why would the crowds turn out for Jesus?

✤ What might Jesus' feelings have been on that day? Did he feel he was 'coming home' to complete his work?

Bible reference: *John 12.12-19*

Pages 20–21 Footprints

Background

Footprints are meant to be followed. Man Friday left a footprint for Robinson Crusoe in Daniel Defoe's *Treasure Island*. Christians try to follow the example set by Jesus, metaphorically placing their feet in his footprints. There is a thirteenth-century story of a small, poorly-dressed man, following exactly in Jesus' footsteps, while important Christian leaders, like bishops and abbots, failed to do so. The small man is St Francis of Assisi. Jesus, whatever is believed about him, left his footprints on time for people to follow.

Ways of using the picture

✤ Ask the pupils about their own footprints. Can they recognize them? Are they distinctive? Do they like making them?

✤ Are they inclined to follow footprints on a beach? What can they imagine of the person who left them? Where were they going? What sort of person were they?

✤ Why do Christians want to follow Jesus' footprints? Jesus didn't actually leave any footprints, so what can Christians try to do in order 'to follow in his footsteps'?

Bible reference: *Luke 6.27-36*

Pages 22–3 Grace Darling to the rescue

Background

Some journeys need incredible courage. Death may be just around the corner, but that simply pushes people on. They may feel at the end of their tether, but they can still carry on; they have a sense of achievement and a sense of hope. Christians believe that Jesus gives them hope in this life and in the life to come. Jesus is the light of the world who lights their way. He is a strong anchor and point of reference in the journey of their lives. The anchor was a symbol used by early Christians to illustrate their faith. The story of Grace Darling in the nineteenth century is a classic tale of courage, selflessness and conviction.

Ways of using the picture

❖ Who, or what, encourages the pupils when they are feeling down?

❖ Who is the strong person, the point of reference in their lives?

❖ Does light bring hope? Why do pupils think Christians use the image of light to refer to Jesus?

Bible references: *John 8.12, Psalm 27.1-5*

Pages 24–5 Icon of the Ascension

Background

Christians believe that Jesus was taken into heaven after he had risen from the dead and appeared to his disciples. By leaving his disciples, he gave them authority as well as responsibility to spread his teaching and teaching about him. He said he would send the Holy Spirit to give his disciples power and authority. Jesus calls the Holy Spirit 'the Comforter', which means that the spirit will urge his followers on, giving them guidance and strength. In the language of the Bible, 'spirit' can mean 'breath' or 'wind', or even 'life'.

Ways of using the picture

❖ When do the pupils believe they were given responsibility to do things?

❖ How do the pupils think the disciples felt when Jesus left them?

❖ When Jesus went away, his disciples couldn't lean on him in the same old way. Was this a good thing? Are the pupils left to do things for themselves? When do they ask for guidance?

❖ Think about why icons are described as 'windows on heaven'.

Bible references: *The Acts of the Apostles 1.6-11, Mark 16.19*

We are grateful to the following for permission to reproduce photographs:

pp. 2–3 Image Bank

p. 4 SuperStock, *Joseph Seeks Lodgings at Bethlehem* by James T. Tissot

pp. 6–7 Bridgeman Art Library/Art Gallery of Western Australia, *Christ in the Wilderness, The Scorpion* by Stanley Spencer

pp. 8–9 Impact Photos/Simon Shepheard

pp. 12–13 John Reilley, artist and photographer, *Jacob's Ladder*

pp. 18–19 and cover Alison Seaman

pp. 20–21 Image Bank

pp. 22–3 Mary Evans Picture Library, *Grace Darling and Papa to the Rescue*

pp. 24–5 and cover The Art Archive, *The Ascension of Christ*, 17th Century Ethiopian Manuscript

Illustrations by:

pp. 10–11 Judy Stevens

pp. 16–17 and cover Peter Dennis/ Linda Rogers Associates

National Society/Church House Publishing
Church House
Great Smith Street
London SW1P 3NZ

ISBN 0 7151 4981 4

Published 2002 by National Society Enterprises Ltd

Copyright © Alan Brown and Alison Seaman 2002

Design: Celia Hart
Picture research: Jane Taylor

Cover design: Julian Smith

Publishing consultant: Joan Ward

Printed by Scotprint, Haddington, East Lothian, Scotland